CROSSCURRENTS

Tony and Claës Lewenhaupt

CROSSCURRENTS

Art • Fashion • Design
1890–1989

RIZZOLI
NEW YORK

Fashion is as distinct a way of interpreting the events and the mood of the times as other cultural statements. The idiom is the same. And nothing is better suited to prove our case than women's clothing of the past century.

Without Christer Strandberg and his fine layout of this book, his ideas, advice, and knowledge of contemporary cultural history, the "crosscurrents" would not have been quite as clear.

Tony and Claës Lewenhaupt
Villa Fortuna
Hälsingborg, Sweden

First published in the United States of America in 1989 by
RIZZOLI INTERNATIONAL PUBLICATIONS, INC.
300 Park Avenue South, New York, NY 10010

Originally published in Swedish under the title *Tidens Tecken* by Förlags AB Wiken

Library of Congress Cataloging-in-Publication Data
Lewenhaupt, Tony.
   Tidens tecken. English
   Crosscurrents: art, fashion, design, 1890–1989 / Tony Lewenhaupt,
Claës Lewenhaupt.
      p. cm.
   Translation of : Tidens tecken.
   ISBN 0-8478-1137-9
   1. Costume—History—19th century. 2. Costume—History—20th
century. 3. Costume design—History—19th century. 4. Costume
design—History—20th century. I. Lewenhaupt, Claës. II. Title.
GT595.L4813 1989
391' .009'04—dc20   89-42921
                                                         CIP

Translated by Jorgen Schiott
Design by Christer Strandberg
Text layout and composition by Blackpool Design/New York
Printed and bound in Italy

C O N T E N T S

Play Of Waves

Meandering nature crept into the history of fashion. Woman's outline settled into a curved stem. Her bosom swelled like a balcony of a house. Her hips undulated like the armrests of chairs. Her skirts wound about her like Victor Horta's staircases. Her hats swayed in the wind like treetops. Her whole body moved in waves like Munch's and Krøyer's sensuous brush strokes. The ideals of a period were reflected in the fashion.

Naturalism's honest resolve gave birth to Art Nouveau. But its style became a decorative package without content. The truth was still hidden inside the corset, under the hem of the skirt, behind the façade, beneath the design, and between the lines.

Reality and Functionalism were certainly already conscious. They could be dimly seen in avant-garde painting, in the architecture of factories, and in discussions of reforming the dress, but their time had not yet come.

Therefore the bewilderingly beautiful trailings and curves of Art Nouveau could tell much about the times, its longings and ideas. Should the style preserve the past or develop the future?

The wife and the home stayed in their locked position but daily papers, trains, and above all the bicycle let the outside world move in closer. Feminism was clamorous, but the tyranny of the corset was tighter than ever. And La Belle Epoque desperately held on to old ideals—wine, women and song—while the Social Democratic Party united the masses in Europe.

The economy was good, and that was what decided how far freedom would be permitted to go. And, consequently, the hemline.

AMPLE BOSOM, exaggerated sway, and sweeping length from the back of the waist give the much-coveted S-silhouette. Look close at the gathered black waist and how it accentuates the curves.

In soft light this spangled tulle dress with its skin-toned undergarments, made in Paris around the turn of the century, must have caused the wearer to appear naked underneath. A glimpse of the double standard typical of the time.

WOMAN QUIETLY insinuated herself into the world of man, dressed on his terms in shirt, tie, long dark unadorned skirt and bootees. Outside the office, the factory, the school, the dressmaker's workshop, or the shop where she worked, she also wore a jacket and a dark or light straw-hat. She knew that she was needed outside the home as well as inside, which gave her a new self-confidence. With this came broader shoulders.

The skirt and blouse were woman's first functional clothes. They therefore served both in the home and workplace, as well as in nature during hours of leisure.

NOTHING MEANT more for the liberation of women than the bicycle. It took her away from the home to work, into nature, toward new freedom. On her bicycle she could move about alone, deciding her own destination and speed. Besides, the bicycle was inexpensive, everyone except the poorest could buy one.

The poster, made in 1889 by Théophile Steinlen for the bicycle firm Comiot, reveals the wavy style both in the shape of the body and in the undulating letters of the text.

THE ART NOUVEAU WOMAN of 1895 was sculptured to perfection. The corset shaped her body, flattened her stomach, lifted her bosom, and tightened her waist, creating the preferred profile. The rest was accomplished by the ample blouse and long skirt, which was always cut in gores or bell-shaped.

This summer ensemble of light wool was cut in a relatively simple manner with a short open jacket showing the important waist and the finely detailed blouse.

THE BROTHERS THONET in Vienna had great success with their light bentwood chairs. During the last decade of the nineteenth century the curves of the chairs were simplified and deepened, as shown by the armrest of this chair.

OVERLEAF: Spain, Belgium, and France represented a freer, more sensual form of Art Nouveau than Scandinavia and Austria, where a less high-flown idiom developed. The façade of this house in Palma de Mallorca is clearly related to Antoni Gaudí's adaptation of Art Nouveau.

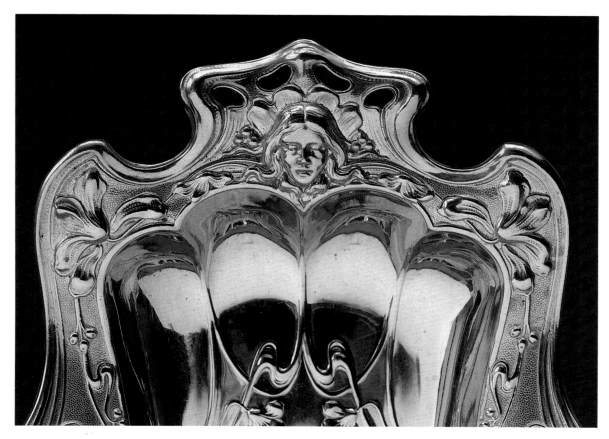

HANDICRAFT MUST GIVE WAY to mass production, even the most complex patterns and shapes.

This particular silver-plated dish has a carefully thought out shape and decoration, but in general mass production with its lack of style wore out Art Nouveau so that it died relatively fast.

THE CORSET had a similar role as mass production: to produce a shape, an ideal.

This corset of double natural-colored and long-wearing linen is buttoned in the front, but laced in the back, and has long, sewn-in, only slightly resilient ribs to further enhance the woman's shape.

OVERLEAF: The trains of the dresses, the outline of the beach, the brush strokes, everything was in harmony, including the newly awakened feeling for a wild and natural landscape. In 1893 Peder Severin Krøyer painted *Summer Evening on Skagen Sønderstrand*. Photographer: Hans Petersen for Den Hirschsprungske Samling, Copenhagen.

THE WHITE BATISTE DRESS from the turn of the century still has the modest high neck, but the sleeves begin to slide up toward the elbow, the puff sleeves are gone, and the silhouette softly straightens.

LIGHT, SOLID-COLORED materials became more popular, and often shades of one color were used for decoration with contrasting materials. The all-white stairway of Otto Wagner's house on Linke Wienzeile in Vienna, constructed 1898–99, was much ahead of its time.

THE TURN of the century arrived with white summer clothes, summer houses, glassed-in verandas, excursions into nature, and a simpler look adorned with unnecessary decorations. The beautiful, extravagant, white wool dress with its inserted gores and pleated chiffon reveals this woman's status.

IN 1903 GUSTAV KLIMT made this sketch as a study for a later portrait. Notice how the folds of the dress lie as a flat pattern within the curving frame outlined by the chair, the dress, and the hair. The three-dimensional idiom of the nineteenth century is becoming two-dimensional.

The First Modernists

The lines of Art Nouveau straightened. They were no longer needed, they had opened the gate to a new way of life and a new mode of expression. The vegetative motif became more and more stylized. Decorations ceased to be mere additions for the sake of social prestige. Designers found inspiration in the Near East, where new discoveries and research drew attention to unknown cultures. The world was gradually knitted together. The railroad, telegraph, telephone, and motion picture brought humanity closer together. The problems were not individual anymore, they became universal.

The picture became more important than the word. It would take a little while before film became a witness of the present, but photography knew no limits. Several women proved themselves as innovative photographers. Illustrated weeklies quickly became common and extremely popular. Still impatience grew. When would freedom in art be realized? Who was doing anything about the injustices of industrialism? What was happening to women's rights? Riots, demonstrations, assassinations, and attempted revolutions, big as well as small, only showed the desperation.

Women's clothes marked the progress of this new era. The skirts were still long, and the waist laced up. Conservatism would not let go. And yet these years were the beginning of the end. The corset was still present, but softening and less demanding. Just as houses, furniture, and household articles straightened into a more controlled shape, woman's outline, too, became less curved. Many architects and other designers found inspiration for the future in the new creativity from Vienna, where Wiener Werkstätte developed novel ideas around form and function, based on an unlimited curiosity about everything from houses to clothes.

The artists formed groups, they manifested themselves. The Futurists were strong and clamorous in their acceptance of the new times: the swiftness, the movement, the speed, the machinery, and the violence. They were proven right.

Cézanne was the first Modernist. What he was to painting, Paul Poiret was to women's fashion. They both knew that it was not enough just to decorate a surface, but that the soul of the thing must be understood and expressed. Braque and Picasso were painting cubistically, and in 1910 Kandinsky produced his first abstract painting. Nature was no longer art. Nature belonged to man, who filled his free time with sentimental poems and home-made handicraft based on flourishing national romanticism.

THE SKIRT was still long, but the neck was bared, and the translucent parts of the waist and the sleeves suggested that the will to nakedness was greater than the convention.

HUES OF GREEN AND GOLD of Art Nouveau reflect the popular enthusiasm for nature. Flowers, leaves, and animals perpetually wind around the sensuous shapes of the flashed glass.

THE SOFTLY DRAWN-OUT PLAY of lines is calm: gentle curves rather than swelling waves.

A new simplicity is felt particularly in the free-cut waist and the single, broad golden gore that gilds the solid-colored, undetailed wool crepe.

OVERLEAF: The designers of Wiener Werkstätte lived in a world of severe and disciplined shapes. Their furniture and interiors seem austere compared to earlier ideals.

At Charlottenlund in Skaane, Sweden, there is a room furnished in 1903 by Koloman Moser. Panels, table, chairs, cabinet, even curtains are clean and simple with little adornment and just a slight curvature of the legs and the back of the chair.

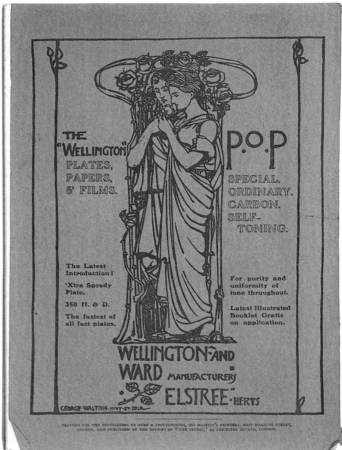

TYPICAL OF THE TIME, an advertisement from 1908 in the periodical *Colour Photography* shows two female figures in classical garments, draped in moderation and with a certain simplification. Even the letters and the layout have a novel softness.

OUTSIDE AND YET INSIDE. The garden was still an area of little interest, but when Art Nouveau ideals were combined with nature, it was only a question of time before horticultural societies became common.

THE PRINTED IRIS PATTERN unfolds in a disciplined fashion. Each bunch is gathered like a dress or the outline of a woman. An anonymous, but good designer in the spirit of the Englishman Charles Voysey.

IN SWEDEN Gunnar G:son Wennerberg of Gustavsberg painted wildflowers on plates, with a light yet realistic touch. He communicated the new simplicity with this wreath of flowers as an expression of Art Nouveau on an otherwise clean plate.

29

ORIGINS WERE SOUGHT in culture as well as nature. National romanticism thrived, in the homestead societies, the regional novel, the open-air museum, the heroic monument, the nature painting, and the wood architecture. Old Norse tracery and symbols became popular and were seen in many contexts, from the reform dress to the Biological Museum in the Deer Park of Stockholm.

The museum was built in 1893 at the request of the conservator and zoologist Gustaf Kolthoff. Designed by Agi Lindegren, it became an early example of a national estheticism that persisted into the twenties.

PROFESSIONAL SPORTS CLOTHES for women did not exist yet. The everyday clothes were supplemented with a knitted jacket or sweater, often handmade. Dressed in this manner, one skated, skied, hiked in the mountains, bicycled, and was sportive in a most general way.

The cardigan, until then a garment for women of the working class, acquired a new status and a pattern that evoked a national romanticism specific for the time.

58

WHEN ARTHUR SJÖGREN illustrated August Strindberg's
Wordplay and Little Art, he imitated with pen and ink the
coveted surface of the woodcut.

A NEST IN THE WILDERNESS was the concept that many
tried to realize by furnishing their summer houses with
stained furniture, handcrafted textiles, open fireplaces, and
windows with small panes.

TWO HOUSES, designed in 1899, built and owned by the architect Otto Wagner on Linke Wienzeile in Vienna. The façades have been smoothed out, and there are no projecting balconies. A restrained order reigns over the eaves and the pilasters, while gold and flowers spread between the windows, around the balconies, and up onto the roof, where one of the goddesses of the Viennese *Jugendstil*, or Art Nouveau, proclaims her triumph.

ANOTHER, similarly tight façade: high-necked, smooth, and long sleeved. A skirt without gathers with a winding indiscreet leaf pattern competing with the deep gold of the waist for attention.

THE ROYAL FOYER of Stockholm's Royal Theater has its own entrance all in white. The banisters of wood and brass are the only added color. A room ahead of its time with an extraordinary feeling for the best of late Art Nouveau.

AROUND 1908–09 the waist moved upward, a classic sign of emancipation. The silhouette straightened, the layers of cloth became translucent, so thin that the shape of the body could be discerned. The adornment is simple and subtle; often gold, but not in vulgar quantities.

This is one of the most beautiful of dresses, unfortunately without label, but much indicates the workshop of Augusta Lundin.

OVERLEAF: One of the few rooms that has been left untouched from the Swedish *Jugendstil* period is at the Royal Theater in Stockholm, built and furnished in 1908. The room of the royal family behind the royal box is Swedish *Jugendstil* at its best: lightness and moderation, with a touch of classical symmetry.

Johan Fredrik Liljekvist is responsible for the architecture and the interior decoration, while the mural was done by Prince Eugen. The motif of the pine trees reoccurs as cones and berries in the detail of furniture and chandeliers.

Probabilities

The modern woman was developed and duplicated. The First World War gave her responsibility. Time granted her the right to vote. Paul Poiret liberated her from the corset. He sensed the atmosphere, understood the need. He knew that woman's patience was at an end. She was only waiting for a sign. In 1909 Poiret showed her how a liberated and self-assured woman could move in his clothes. The outline was loosened, became straight and free; the clothes floated around the body and were held together by soft belts or cords somewhere between the bosom and the waist. The neck was visible as well as the elbows and ankles.

Furniture, too, was given arms and legs. Padding and fringes disappeared. As a body long concealed, the true shapes of the furniture appeared beneath the new electrical lights of the drawing-room. The wooden surfaces shone in their nakedness. Furnishings became obvious, as did the buttons and the pockets of the clothes. Houses, clothes, interiors, household articles, everything—even the ideas—went through a liberating purification; and the necessary details that were so discreet before, now became prominent and conspicuous. The trend would manifest itself little by little as Functionalism.

At the same time there was a growing longing for another world, filled with classical beauty, untouched cultures, and romantic excitement. The exotic was praised. The success of the Ballets Russes was inevitable. Persia, Egypt, and North Africa inspired the whole avant-garde from Matisse to D. W. Griffith.

The motion picture was an escape from reality. The epics of the big screen allowed people to forget for a while the documentary's reports from the alarmingly real war.

But what was happening in Russia after the October Revolution?

And when would the tango end? Like a perpetual hot sensuous wind it blew across the world.

A RAISED WAIST was a classic sign of female emancipation. The reduction in the amount of fabric used and the bare neck, as in this silk dress from 1912, were also typical language of the times. The years before the First World War were important for the feminist movement, which now had a goal in sight.

ROMANTIC EXOTICISM is displayed by the Poiret-inspired evening dress from 1913, with draped skirt, tassels, and a magnificently embroidered waist in vivid colors.

OTTO WAGNER'S gleaming golden high altar from 1907 in Kirche am Steinhof outside Vienna has a clearly exotic, oriental feeling, too, both in design and decoration.

LARGE BUCKLES and decorative buttons were used together with tassels and ball fringes as isolated but conspicuous details between 1910 and 1914–15.

Harem romanticism was found just as often in the interiors as in the clothing. Low divans with tasseled cushions adorned many homes.

THE ORIENT as seen by the West and by the world of fashion. A piece of lamé in a color combination worthy of the Fauvists.

THE SUCCESS of the Ballets Russes confirmed the fascination of the time for the exotic. The ballet *Schéhérazade* and Léon Bakst's innovative dance costumes are considered to have influenced fashion and Paul Poiret greatly.

The costumes of Schéhérazade can now be seen in the collection of the Museum of Dance in Stockholm. Time has faded the colors, but not Bakst's sensational mixture of the Baroque and Oriental.

DARING COLOR COMBINATIONS, large demonstrative details and a raised waist were typical of the years before the First World War.

The evening dress of thin georgette is cut with a few bold strokes, which contributes a sensual softness.

AROUND 1910–12 the ideal feminine shape is straightened. Trimmings lie on the outside of a simple base in a decorative pattern.

Detailing in black is common, always conspicuous and against a contrasting background, as on this dress of blue silk.

THIS PREDILECTION for black detail against a severe background can be found on and around the doors of Otto Wagner's villa, which he built for his own use in 1912 on Hüttelbergstrasse in Vienna.

RESTRAINT came with Neoclassicism and its purity of form. White clothes, high waist, classical borders and details became fashionable.

The dress from 1912–13 in white empire-inspired silk reveals how quickly the liberation from the corset, the floor-length, wide skirt, and the long, narrow sleeves occurred.

THE SHAPE OF PERFUME BOTTLES always echoes the prevailing fashion. The fashion designer Molyneux's faceted column-shaped bottle is typical of the period.

IN ENGLAND Ambrose Heal worked as a pioneer in home environment and interior design.

His furniture was free of status symbols. Calm and sober, with allowance for a little friendly decoration that fulfilled its function at the same time, he produced a series of fine, basic furniture, something entirely new for the time.

THE HIKING SUIT in heavy green cotton has a jacket that is not unlike a military jacket with its turn-up collar, capacious pockets, practical straps, wind-tight double buttoning, and unornate belt.

With the First World War woman definitively entered the man's world, demonstrated by her sports clothes. In the jacket the label says "Aug. Schultz Ystad" which indicates that the suit was bought ready to wear. This, too, was something new for a social class that had plenty of free time.

A FRUGAL, BUT COMFORTABLE INTERIOR for a Swedish house created in 1917–18 by Heal & Co. of London.

The furniture and the textiles have an almost rural character with their clean wood surfaces. The vertically elongated design recurs in the work of several important designers during this period, such as Charles Rennie Mackintosh, the backs of whose chairs are sometimes tall as ladders.

Notice also that a pronounced asymmetrical arrangement of the furniture begins to appear.

A MOST INTERESTING DRESS from 1917, made from broadcloth by the fashion house Jeanne Pène in Paris.

The neck is bare, conspicuously naked, and the skirt is relatively short. While the waistline is subtly emphasized, the dress as a whole falls loose and free, revealing the embroidered silk lining, even more so when the woman moves.

The asymmetry is striking and relevant to the time, as is the color combination of claret, ocher, clear blue—an expressionistic dress.

FLAT, SHADOWLESS PATTERNS with Cubistic feeling and excessive black were typical of Wiener Werkstätte's production.

A NEW SIMPLICITY appeared with the First World War. There was neither will, occasion, or means for extravagance or anything unnecessary.

As women took responsibility for the home front, their clothes were simplified, becoming functional and free.

Above all, the skirts became shorter and were cut to allow a more comfortable walking width. This attractive cotton dress with white batiste collar is a dress for an active woman.

OTTO WAGNER'S Post Office Savings Bank in Vienna, 1903–12, shows the intention of many artists of the time to simplify and clarify function and form.

The details of construction are emphasized, the façade is flattened, and angles replace curves. The materials become cool, hygienic, and unsensual. Aluminium and tile are modern materials that do not pretend to be what they are not.

THE SAME IDEOLOGY is expressed in the interior of the
Post Office Savings Bank. An offical room with a clearly
indicated purpose. The presence of the radiators is strongly accentuated, as are the bolts of the walls. The color
range is restrained and the walls are decorated only by a
black-and-white mosaic band.

THE TENDENCY TO ABSTRACT and isolate surrounding objects is revealed by one of the first Cubists, Georges Braque, in *Still Life with Violin*. Collection: The National Museum, Stockholm.

WITH TIME fashion became more and more Cubistic—simplified in form, color, and outline. The black of the evening cape is broken only by the contrast between velvet and silk, no details are allowed.

1919–1928
Two Dimensions

During these animated, restless years the grown-ups played. They danced, frequented night clubs, listened to jazz, drank cocktails, and favored black artists. Sex was discussed openly in books, on stage, in film, and sometimes even in real life. Birth control became a public matter.

But why did the liberated woman hide in the disguise of the tomboy, *la garçonne*? Was the time not ripe? She was curious like a child, and thus dressed like one in straight frock and strap shoes. Her hair was bobbed, and she had neither bosom nor waist. Many women lived in blinkers. To them the fastest car, the newest hit song, the latest movie, the reddest lipstick, and the most lavish party composed the essentials of life. They lived as mindlessly as they were dressed. With time their clothes became more and more childish and the skirts shorter and shorter. The distinction between child and woman became nonexistent. The boundaries between art and design were also obliterated, similarly between private sphere and public sphere, light music and serious music, ballet and dance, theater and fashion . . .

Cubism suited the atmosphere of the period. Underneath the flat surface there was nothing. Cubism is two-dimensional, just as angular and shadowless as the clothing. In architecture as well, the ornate façade was forgotten, the wall of the house became plain, flat as a dress. In Russia the Constructivists lived with their abstract cubist ideals, while De Stijl, the Dutch group in the same spirit, worked in a concentrated manner using the colors of Modernism: blue, red, yellow, white, and black. The ideas of De Stijl became important for the Bauhaus, the school of design that was formed in Weimar in 1919 and which in its turn became important for Functionalism and for the role of the designer in the industrial society. While the Bauhaus was more concerned with form and function than with attractive appearance, a decorative and accessible style was developed, soon dominating everything from book covers to furniture. Art Deco was born and christened at the *Exposition des Arts Décoratifs* in Paris 1925. It became a sometimes well-digested, but often slapdash mixture of dressed-up Cubism, anything Chinese, and newly discovered Egyptian history.

The real world, of course, was quite different. High inflation in Germany. Civil war in Russia and Ireland. Prohibition in the United States and general strike in England. As soon as peace was established, unrest returned. In Italy Mussolini gathered his Blackshirts, and in Germany Hitler dressed his men in brown. The colors of patriotism darkened.

Wall Street collapsed on October 24, 1929. "I ain't got nobody," lamented Bessie Smith.

THE CAR BECAME COMMON and, consequently, the car coat. Functional and comfortable with pronounced and practical detail.

THE SERENITY of this silk dress is broken only by the curved line of the hat and the tunic. An exquisite example—in light, silk georgette—of fashion in transition between the curvy, feminine teens and the flat, masculine twenties.

IN GUNNAR ASPLUND'S COURTHOUSE, built in 1921, in Sölvesborg, all surfaces are clean and smooth with a few but essential details, often in a friendly curved shape that alleviates the severity of atmosphere and color.

NO WAIST, no bosom, no hips: the fashion of the twenties was based on cubistic and geometric ideals. The dress, a sophisticated frock, is sewn in thin blue silk with drawn-thread work to emphasize angularity and a white collar to underscore the childishness.

THE CONCERT HALL in Stockholm from 1926, typical of the time and of the architect Ivar Tengbom, combines a geometric simplicity with a feeling for the grandiose.

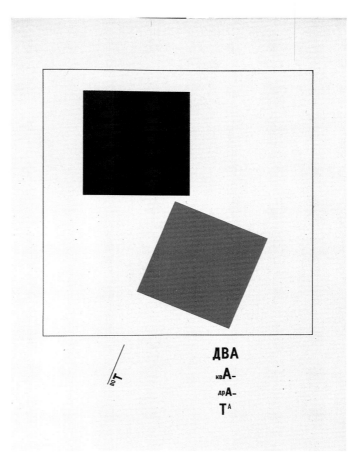

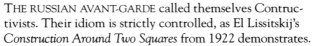

THE RUSSIAN AVANT-GARDE called themselves Contructivists. Their idiom is strictly controlled, as El Lissitskij's *Construction Around Two Squares* from 1922 demonstrates.

AFTER THE REVOLUTION of 1917, the creative groups in Russia enjoyed great artistic freedom, which spurred a short period of advanced experimentation. Art was supposed to reach the people, but mass production did not succeed.
   This outfit by artist Malevich was never manufactured, but Carina Pogoldh has sewn a faithful copy.

THE DE STIJL GROUP in Holland with Piet Mondrian, Gerrit Rietveld, and Theo van Doesburg among others, declared that "the machine is a result of spiritual discipline." Rietveld's experiments with simplified forms of chairs was clearly ahead of the times.
   This well-known chair was already made in 1919.

ART DECO is characterized by abstract geometric patterns, which spread everywhere in the private as well as the public environments. Black and gold were a slightly decadent combination fitting for the taste of the time for luxury and night life.

The evening cloak, sewn at an unknown French fashion house, is cut as clean as a bath robe.

CHRISTIAN BERG'S streamlined, rather flat-chested feminine ideal from 1926 is quite in the spirit of the time, and furthermore is dressed in gold and black.

IN PARIS the artistic freedom was limitless and very productive. There, the young generation, Picasso, Léger, Dufy, and Cocteau, competed at creating scenography and stage costumes as well as textile prints, clothes, and jewelry.

Sonia Delaunay used both geometric motifs and African primitivism in her patterns, translating them into clothing and stage costumes. Her patterns appear in the book *Compositions et Idées* from 1925.

AROUND 1924–25 the dress functioned as a smooth plane on which the pattern, often inspired by African art, was embroidered or printed.

The black silk foundation with steely shining metal embroidery shows at the same time that Functionalism was not far off.

KANDINSKY'S ABSTRACT cubism deals with shadowless
geometric shapes. The same idiom can be seen in fashion
and in the feminine ideal.

TO COMPARE THE COLD, precise design of this piece of jewelry by Harald Nielsen with the natural curves of Art Nouveau demonstrates how quickly styles change.

SURFACES decorated with flat oriental patterns can be hard such as stone, like the fountain in the town park of the French town Isle-sur-la-Sorgue.

ORIENTALISM sought inspiration further and further away. Japan and China with their traditional clean surfaces and controlled ornamentation suited the twenties perfectly. The combination of the pleated skirt and the hip-length blouse was common but sometimes so exclusive that it was sewn in silk with Chinese gold embroideries.

AMÉDÉE OZENFANT'S painting *Composition*, 1929, shows how severe Cubism began to give way to rounded and mature shapes. Collection: Statens Konstmuseer, Stockholm.

SLEEVES, COLLAR, skirt, waist, bosom, everything disappeared around 1924–25. All that remained was a childlike copy of the idol Theda Bara, who tried to appear worldly-wise and world-weary in her hunt for diversions.

Never before did people dance for so long, so often, and with such abandon. The Charleston fever raged, men and women let go of each other, and the clothes marked the beat through embroidery, pleats, fringes, and flounces that swung from the hips.

Compare with the sixties and the twist: both decades expressed new sexual freedom in minimal clothing. Most of the woman's body was freely exposed—note the flesh-colored stockings.

Many pearl-embroidered small, black, silk dresses were preserved from this time, but this one, with its gray arabesques, is among the most beautiful.

IN EMBROIDERY OR RAILROAD TRACKS, it made no difference, patterned images recurred. All that mattered was conspicuous clarity and flatness.

In 1927 the artist Cassandre made this poster, which demonstrates the new status of the train as the means for fast and far-off adventures.

ART DECO spread into the applied arts. The fountain in the small French town of Goult is from 1928 and shows how far and how deep the inspiration reached.

THE SURFACE became smoother and smoother. The body became a screen upon which fashion was projected.

This thin silk casing is from the fashion house of Henriette Boudreau in Paris.

OVERLEAF: Uncompromising Functionalism marks Josef Frank's house in Falsterbo from 1927. The deck house on top and the rail of the terrace bring a cruise ship to mind, something that is quite intentional and very characteristic of the period.

Doubtful News

The skirt fell together with the Stock Exchange. Depression and unemployment followed as did dark, modest clothes. Subjectively established values and opinions became worthless. A new collective morality showed the way to a lighter future. "A New Deal," Roosevelt promised. Reason spoke. And Functionalism answered. Forget status symbols and pasted-on decorations. Think clean, free, and simple. What is functional is always beautiful.

The artists were pessimists, they saw the absurdity of a split existence and expressed their feelings through Surrealism. And as the thirties went by, the real world became more and more similar to the world of Surrealism.

But the architects and the designers were optimists. They believed in a whitewashed and well-organized future filled with air and light and built from new materials; rational houses that opened up to the great solidarity. The shapes of Functionalism were just as simple and smooth as the women's clothes. The outline of the new fashion was like the new typography: clear and sharp without frills and modifications. A convincing simplicity resting on a carefully worked-out foundation. Seams were not to be seen in clothing, lettering, or furniture. Totality was what mattered.

The confidant working woman was free to make her own decisions and was heard and seen in fashion, film, daily life, the sports field, and in the air. Greta Garbo was the idol, Amelia Earhart the pioneer . . .

Along with the new threat of war, a tougher feminine ideal appeared. The suit was the woman's uniform, with broad, padded shoulders, and a hard, determined expression to show her preparedness. She was needed, for the thirties were to end in a nightmare where Hitler's lust for power threatened all hope for a future.

Many felt alienated in an existence that got better for some only through worsening conditions for others and sought protection and distraction in a fantasy world filled with masquerades, musicals, romanticized epic films, historical fashion, and surrealistic hats. More and more people traveled in order to calm their restlessness; but, traveling was more a diversion than a necessity, a way of experiencing something new—freedom and sun. The evening dress became very décolleté in the back in order to show off the tan, and the everyday clothes acquired a professional sportiveness suggesting endless and voluntary leisure.

With the rearmament the conjectures rose, and the skirt followed!

NEVER, neither before nor afterwards, were women's clothes so sexy, so filled with genuine femininity, as during the first half of the thirties. They accentuated the body without clinging and emphasized the curves without exaggerating; they suggested, but revealed nothing.

Madeleine Lemoine's supreme black evening dress has neither waist, back, lining, buttons, nor zipper.

VILLA EDSTRAND in Falsterbo, Sweden, designed in 1935 by Sigurd Lewerentz, has large windows that allow maximum exposure.

The geometric simplicity of the dining-room interior is striking and sophisticated, emphasized by the blackness of the dining table, the mirrored surface of the tea cart, and the light of the floor lamp which defines the hard angles.

LIGHT AND SUN penetrated the world of fashion as well as homes. Increased travel led to sun worship, and the lowcut backs of the evening dresses became as common as the sun terraces of the villas.

GEOMETRIC COMPONENTS, full of unexpected angles and well-lit rooms, comprise Sven Markelius's white concert hall in Helsingborg, 1932. The new architecture suited city people, who had to live in close proximity to each other, but who still wanted the feeling of freedom in the heart of a concentrated society.

A LONG, UNIFIED OUTLINE, geometrically simple details and patterns: women's clothes in the beginning of the thirties were like the architect's houses.

The woman in her discreet, well-made, white linen suit is light years removed from the rather frivolous tomboy of the twenties, in lifestyle as well as looks.

OVERLEAF: Space and light have been added without changing the shape of the room. The mirrored walls reflect the intention of the architect. In Sven Markelius's concert hall the semi-circular cloakroom galleries surround a large stairway. The shape and the mirrors combined give an unexpected sensualism to the austere gray-black room.

THE UNDERSTATED ELEGANCE that made discretion a point of honor suited the early thirties, when nobody wished to show lack of solidarity by flaunting success or wealth. Long black dresses were legion. Precious jewelry, embroidery, and conspicuous detail were replaced by geometrically shaped buttons and buckles of mirror glass or Babbitt metal, or by nothing at all.

THE IDEAL INTERIOR of Functionalism must suit eveyone and be entirely free of implied social status, with only standardized and necessary components: in total, a habitation machine. Mirrors replaced the status of gilding, and mirrored tables, screens, and walls became important elements in interiors that needed light.

THE CATALOGUE for the Stockholm Exhibition in 1930 shows the style of the time: asymmetry, clarity, purity. The layout looks new and modern just like the simple coloration.

Gunnar Asplund, the architect of the exhibition, was responsible for the catalogue, while the sharp wing, the symbol of the exhibition, was drawn by Sigurd Lewerentz.

COMMUNICATION must be clear, says Moholy-Nagy speaking of typography, but the statement could refer to most media including that of fashion.

The clothes of the early thirties with their clean lines were similar to the new lettering that was created by Paul Renner among others. The black silk dress with the tight-fitting hat as a finishing touch has the same shadowless outline as the new Futura typeface, used on the book's cover.

NEW MATERIALS and improved production led to standardized housing. In 1930 Karl-Marx-Hof in the working-class quarters of Vienna was completed. A monumental group of buildings in functionalistic style with towers, flagpoles, allegorical figures, spacious lawns, and an overall idealism. The architect was Karl Ehn.

EVERYDAY LIFE was simplified and functionalized, which also entailed that the wardrobe be more uniform. Skirt and blouse or skirt and sweater became everyday clothes for everyone.

Terra-cotta and ocher shades were used in fabrics as well as in the buildings. They became a logical development of the grayish black tones.

THE TUBULAR STEEL CHAIR appears simple: a frame in which two black plates rest. But look closer at the joints, and they show the same richness in construction as the dress.

Chairs and clothing must fit the body, not the other way around. Marcel Breuer did not design this particular chair, but his similar creation of 1925 gained popularity, and in the thirties more or less faithful replicas of Breuer's tubular steel furniture appeared in many public spaces, where their cool simplicity was shown to their advantage.

UPON CLOSE EXAMINATION the black crepe dress has such an intricate and innovative cut that the seams slanting across hips and waist create a flawless whole, unbroken by detail, but accentuated by the narrow border of silver-plated leather around the neck.

One of the great fashion designers of the thirties, Jeanne Lanvin of Paris, is the author of this work, dated around 1935. Note the shoulders have begun to broaden.

GRADUALLY the clothing industry struck out on new paths and tried in particular to fill the need for leisure wear with its own ideas. In this area the dressmakers had little experience, nor did they have any concept of comfort or adaptation to the surroundings.

A few blue buttons, a couple of embroidered anchors, and plain white cotton piqué are sufficient to give this Swedish-made dress from the middle of the thirties a look of the outdoors.

THE ARCHITECTS of Functionalism cherished light-colored façades, many large openings, sunny terraces, balconies, and flat roofs. The houses resembled stranded ocean liners.

At Klampenborg outside of Copenhagen lies Arne Jacobsen's Bellavista, a group of housing units built between 1932 and 1934.

THE PLATE RISES to a scalloped edge. The black, shiny surface is carried over from Functionalism and is complimented by the new stainless-steel utensils for everyday use.

CLOTHES became theatrical, exaggerated in shape and decoration. Like the motion picture, fashion often found inspiration in the past. Particularly the sixteenth and seventeenth centuries were looked upon as romantic periods filled with divinely beautiful ladies and brave knights.

Toward the end of the thirties the feminine form became more conventionally sexy. Look at the snug long waist, which is entirely covered with spangles, while the skirt is a single flared flounce of tulle.

The hat shows the new interest in separately conceived hats. Original designs that have no direct relation to the clothes, but live their own, often surrealistic, life.

THE CAR was given a new streamlined shape. As always, Citroën was far ahead in design and concept. Their *Berliner-modell* had strong rounded features corresponding to the fashion of the period, as revealed by this toy car.

EQUALITY was achieved first in the area of leisure, then at work, and lastly at home. Long pants belonged to a sporty look that became an everyday outfit during a time of rationing of firewood, coal, and stockings.

The Tyrolese inspiration evident in the color and pattern of this comfortable outfit is attributed to the popularity of things German up until the end of the thirties.

THE WEEKEND COTTAGE and the summer cottage soon turned into leisure houses to be used year round, with open fireplaces and simple, solid interior design of light natural materials.

This interior from one of Josef Frank's houses in Falsterbo shows the most important room of the house, which is simultaneously entrance, hallway, living room, and dining room. The new rounded form from the middle of the thirties can be seen in the mantel of the fireplace, the stairway, and the flowered pattern of the curtain.

To Be Continued

Chaplin's *The Dictator* was released in 1940. In 1945 Evelyn Waugh published *A Lost World*. From the point of view of the arts the war became a period of suspension, an intermission. The Nazi occupation cut off creativity in several countries. Ideas and projects dried up. Instead, temporary and often over explicit ideals appeared, easily perceived and understood in a chaotic society.

Details and shapes were simplified and magnified. Information became unambiguous, the discussion one-sided.

Woman became the Earth Mother with heavily accentuated and rounded bosom and hips. Hats and hair styles were high, shoulders broad and padded, masculine long pants replaced the longed-for stockings, and skirts became short and efficient. Woman had to present herself as big and strong, worthy of the task of defending the home front and the daily life of the family.

Furniture, cars, household articles, and typography received the same emphasized form as the women. The spare, rationed reality was hidden underneath drapings, paddings, trailing plants, conspicuous patterns, and splashy texts. The ingenuity of the time to create something out of nothing was as evident in women's hats as in their soup pots.

Radio and film were important media. Film provided information, diversion, and new courage. The morality of the films was clear, their heroes and heroines as black and white as the cinematography. The long dark shadows underscored intentions and moods.

New York became the new, free, creative welcome center. Jackson Pollack's wild Abstract Expressionism communicated the anger that existed in many confused and war-weary people.

Peace was established in 1945. The newly formed United Nations was to guarantee freedom of thought, word, and action.

At the same time the first nuclear bomb was dropped.

THE MAN'S SUIT was the source of the basic garment of these war-torn years, the custom-made suit, which stressed function rather than appearance. This suit's label says "Perfect Tailoring."

The hat became a protest against rationing, horror, and restrictions. The heavily decorated, spontaneous creations were fashion's contribution to Surrealism.

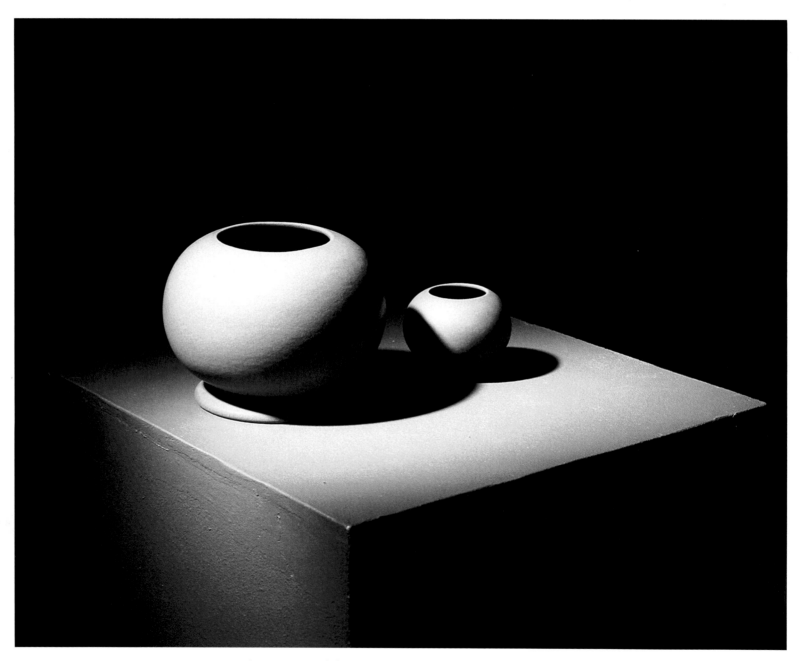

ROUND SHAPES give an impression of generosity and therefore became common during the years of the war.

MANY HATS were set at a new angle that accentuated the face and the expression. The heavy make-up with emphasized eyebrows and a big red mouth did the rest.

THIS LIGHTER has no decoration that would have increased its price or the amount of material needed. "Victory" delivers the right moral message.

MANY WOMEN lived in uniform. Others showed their solidarity by dressing in clothes that imitated the uniforms in color, detail, and, preferably, materials.

OVERLEAF: In order to compensate for lack of materials, furniture and interiors developed a puffed look and, with time, a more asymmetrical shape. The wooden details are covered with glossy varnish and steel springs replace down and horsehair; a kind of false solidity that is seen in many other areas as well.

FERNAND LÉGER'S PORTRAIT of 1942 shows the feminine ideal of the war years: decisive, firm, and physically daring. All the soft romanticism and meekness is gone.

ELSA SCHIAPARELLI understood the new role of women better than any other fashion designer. She became the first to dress women in odd jackets with few but functional and decorative accessories.

ONE HUNDRED AND TWELVE fashion houses remained open in Paris during the occupation, but their new creations reached other countries only by detours. Instead, the inspiration came from Hollywood, where the movie stars became fashion models as well.

The glamorous lamé dress has both Joan Crawford's and the era's signals built into its clearly accentuated and improved silhouette.

THE SAME OUTLINE recurs in Schiaparelli's perfume bottle for Shocking Pink.

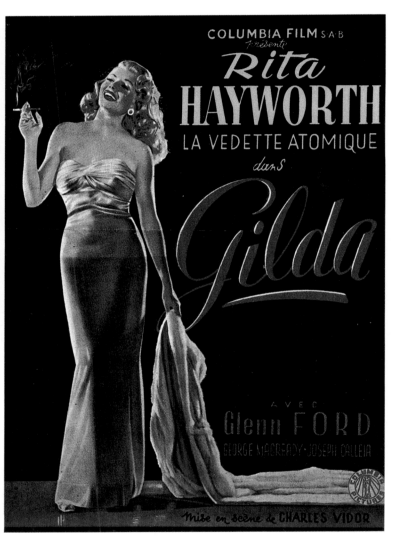

RITA HAYWORTH in the film *Gilda* has everything desired by men and women: sexiness, toughness and self-confidence.

RECORD SLEEVES, book covers, and wrapping in general all displayed the same catchy texts and illustrations that tried to convey a smooth and modern American impression.

SECOND-RATE WARTIME MATERIALS were masked by splashy and contrasting patterns that aimed at giving a handpainted impression.

SCHIAPARELLI'S TALC POWDER PACKAGING resembles an idealized dress dummy.

THE SUIT became indispensable, for everyday use it was gray or brown, on special occasions, black.

This black suit, signed Paquin, and the hat from Claude St. Cyr, both of Paris, show the nostalgic tendencies at the end of the war years, expressed in bustlelike effects and drapings which, in their turn, demonstrate the curvier outline.

Cultural Collisions

When Dior showed his New Look in the spring of 1947, it was an event full of symbolism. The strong responsible look now gave way to a fragile and conservative feminine ideal. The shoulders dropped, the waist was constricted, the skirts became longer, and discussion of equality ceased . . . unfortunately quite voluntarily. Security was to be found in what was long past, long before the Second World War.

Contradictory ideas collided as the fifties approached. The gap between men and women increased. Having been backed by the population during the war, the authorities now lost their grip. Communism versus anti-communism, realism versus escapism, realistic British dramas versus romantic Broadway musicals, or Abstact Expressionism versus national romanticism. Only Existentialism was unambiguous—black and gloomily intellectual.

But a new generation was emerging, looking ahead with optimism and back in anger and irritation. The young wanted to create their own culture and did so, strongly influenced by the "beat" generation. Within a couple of years they were heard and seen more than anyone else. James Dean became their idol and the motorcycle just as important a means of communication as rock'n'roll.

The young made new demands on the mass culture. The industry had to become creative and up-to-date, which included the clothes industry, too. In order to demonstrate their competitive power, countries competed at showing their new "image" at festivals and fairs with prestigious architecture which had rarely anything in common with the hurried construction projects of the time.

Architects became engineers and urban planners, while the new designers of the industry forgot the functionalistic and nostalgic ideals. The streamlined shape was the future.

The asymmetrical shape of the boomerang was perceived as liberating. Like the first space capsule, Sputnik I, or the molecular system of the atom, the boomerang moved freely, but purposefully in space. Space began to be comprehensible and therefore inspiring.

For the first time in history it was the young generation that created the expression of the time and consequently fashion. The new French wave in film belonged to the young, as did the sprawling texts of advertising, Elvis Presley's appeal, blue jeans, T-shirts, elastic belts, ballerina shoes, butterfly chairs, coffee houses, jukeboxes, and money. The economy was booming; everyone who wanted to work could get a job and along with it came money and leisure.

War, politics, and parents were history and who cared about that . . . there was TV!

THE TWO-PIECE OUTFIT in black mat jersey and the ballerina buckled shoes in black mocha are original Dior from 1947.

NEW ELASTIC PANTS had the same intention as the tubular steel legs of furniture: to contrast quite deliberately the organic design of the seat, the tabletop, or the upper body.

THE BLACKENED AND SPRAWLING PLAYFULNESS that liberated typography and illustrations from the monotonous splashiness of the war period was quickly discovered by the graphic industries. Olle Eksell's cover for *Venus i Köket* ("Venus in the Kitchen") is a fine example from 1953.

THE EXISTENTIALISTS of Paris were quite dark. Their intellectual melancholy was different and exciting to the young, who got their first voluntary uniform through them: polo shirt, long pants, ballerina shoes, and winter duffel coat.

ANGULAR ASYMMETRY and streamlined shape were two ideals that were often combined in the same object. New materials and techniques also simplified the furniture, such as this chair of molded plywood from 1953, The Ant, by Arne Jacobsen.

THE CURVED SHAPE of the chair was the same as the feminine form. Solid black recurred in the suit as well, "the little black number" of the fifties. This particular one was made by Hettemarks.

THE URGE TO ACCENTUATE the elongated asymmetric and, at the same time, strongly dynamic shapes was the same for both the conscious as well as the unconscious designer. The woman who painted her eyes with broader slanting lines followed her intuition, while the architect Le Corbusier recognized the desire for a future free of nostalgia.

When he created the church Notre Dame du Haut in Rochamp in the early fifties, he abandoned cold functionalism for a warm, very free sensualism.

THIS WRAPAROUND TOP whether in turquoise, black, or orange shows how the important odd-piece fashion began to acquire status and how the acute triangle became a common shape in many areas during the fifties.

CONCRETE REALISM, in contrast to Abstract Expressionism, manifested itself primarily in Scandinavia. After 1954, Olle Baertling often worked with contrasting angles, which recurred in large wall paintings as well as in smaller serigraphs.

THE BOYISH BLOUSE came from the new design consciousness of the ready-wear industry and not from the fashion houses of Paris. The silhouette retained its conservative femininity, but the clothes were about to lose in elegance what they would gain in freedom and youthfulness.

NEW IDEAS appeared in all areas of industry. The Gense flatware in polished stainless steel and black plastic, design by Folke Arström, has a deliberate status-free style.

CLEAR AND PRECISE TRIANGLES were seen everywhere around 1954–55. Stig Lindberg's ashtray, Domino, from Gustavsberg is typical of the time.

NYLON CLOTHES were new and ironing forgotten. Both this style and pattern originated in the United States, about 1950.

ABSTRACT EXPRESSIONISM helped make New York the new artistic metropolis of the western world. The painting, *Untitled*, 1956, is by Sam Francis. Collection: Louisiana, Denmark.

SUNGLASSES were streamlined and pointed like the eyes of a cat or the stroke of eyeliner. Audrey Hepburn was the idol.

LEISURE HOURS were filled with plastic furniture—lightweight, cheap, and functional with its stripped-status freedom.

LONG TAIL-FINS were meant to stress the rocketlike speed of
the Chevrolet Impala 1959 model.

ARCHITECTURE emphasized the feeling of the time for mass communication and transportation. Many buildings had the character of an airport or gas station.

MANY INTERIORS showed the desire to forget the old stylistic ideals that were still noticeable in other areas. Look at this Swedish, very consistent, and intensely colored interior, created in 1955 for a villa in Falsterbo. Not one line runs parallel with another, but there is no cautious commercialism, either.

YOUNG WOMEN wanted clothing to suit their lifestyle and the image of "a lady" was not what they had in mind! Mary Quant was the first to understand, then some foresighted clothing manufacturers realized the extent of the message, and Ivar Wahl in Sweden made this sleeveless outfit with matching coat in cotton jersey in a daring color combination.

Space Proximity

To be middle-aged was as depressing as believing in God. Jesus Christ was more successful as a musical. John F. Kennedy, Andy Warhol, and the Beatles were the idols who caught attention. They expressed themselves in uncomplicated and easily understood slogans, refrains, clichés, and cartoons.

Space research was just as unambiguous: it had no history, only a future.

The architects built terrestrial space stations with glass walls and antennae. In the world of fashion clothes were perpetually white, spatially functional, and synthetic. The industrial designers loved the unlimited possibilities of plastic, which suited the impatient consumer society. "Buy, wear, and throw away" went for everything from white plastic boots to space capsules.

The young continued to create their own culture, their own morality, and their own day and night. Discotheques were more fun than school, sexual technique was as popular as science fiction, and London was the center of the world.

The pill gave women freedom and equality, which she accentuated with miniskirts, long pants, and bare breasts.

There was war in Vietnam, Rachel Carson wrote *Silent Spring*, and in China Mao carried out his cultural revolution.

Reality was only felt when it was too late.

WOMEN of the space age dressed in white clothes and low flat boots. On the way to the moon both bosom and waist disappeared, leaving only a childlike frock. The future looked good, and the skirts were short. The dress in thick white wool is from Geral, Paris.

OVERLEAF: Sten Samuelson's building of 1967 for Frigoscandia outside of Helsingborg looks like a space station. The glass walls, the aluminum plates, and the thin concrete columns strengthen the impression.

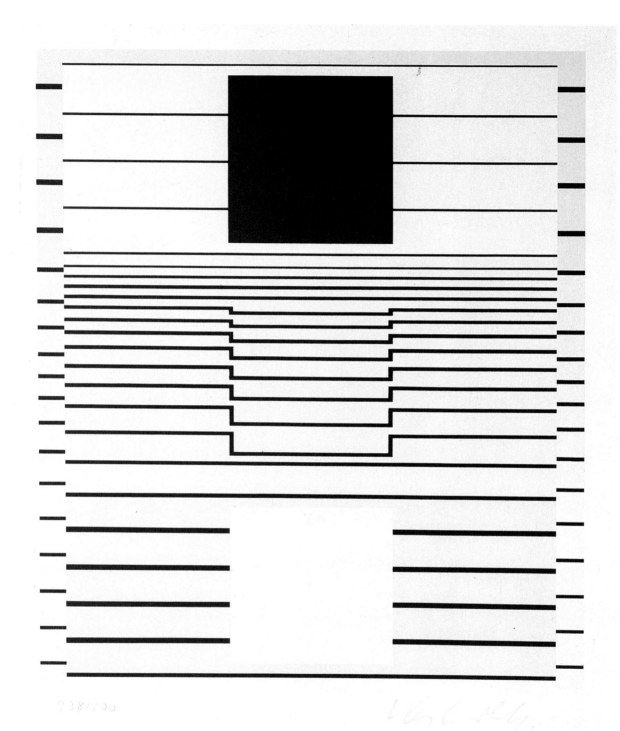

OP ART became the logical continuation of the Concrete Realism of the fifties. Victor Vasarely was one of its most outstanding artists and quickly became famous thanks to the increasing importance of mass media and its efficient communication of the expressions of the time.

OF COURSE OP ART moved into the world of fashion, where it played with proportion and shapes. Like several other designers in 1965, Katja of Sweden presented a black-and-white collection.

OVERLEAF: Philip Johnson's promenade in the State Theater, Lincoln Center, New York. In the center is Elie Nadelman's sculpture *Two Female Nudes*, around them anonymous silhouettes seem to float in the universe on weightless platforms, the lighting creating new worlds.

THE POSSIBILITIES of plastic lured the great designers like Charles Eames, Verner Panton, and Eero Saarinen, who often worked with chairs in soft shapes and cast plastic.

This particular stackable chair, however, is from Østergaard in Denmark.

CAST IN ONE PIECE, safe, always retaining its shape, and with no pretensions to add expense, the plastic bottle replaced the metal container.

BY 1966 ANDRÉ COURRÈGE'S DECREE to wear long pants had reached all women, and with relief they washed, dried, and wore their new clothes of plastic and synthetics.

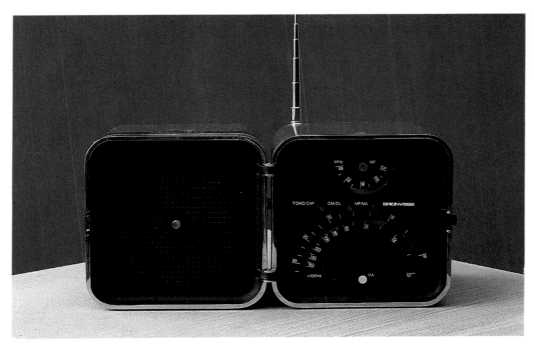

THE FUTURISTIC FUNCTIONAL DESIGN was dominated by the Italian furniture designers, who also manufactured smaller articles for everyday use, like telephones, lamps, and ashtrays. Brionvega's portable compact radio from 1964 was designed by Marco Zanuso and Richard Sapper.

THE WHITE JUMPSUITS of the space fashion were replaced by men's suits—equal and tough with shiny steel heels, neck tie and man's hat.

OVERLEAF: Andy Warhol was the mass consumer's, the comics reader's, and the idol worshipper's creative interpreter. When Marlon Brando, dressed in leather, was established as the big city idol, Warhol made this portrait in 1966, titled *Four Marlons*. Collection: Louisiana, Denmark.

THE CLASSIER THE ENVIRONMENT, the greater the occasion to protest against capitalism and the upper class. There was little true solidarity between the working class and protesters. However, tribute was paid to blue-collar workers: their clothes became the fashion for demonstrators. But the undershirt was given color, and the jeans, wide legs and low cut.

Alarm Clocks

The student revolt in Paris became the spark that set the movement on fire. On both sides of the Atlantic, there were protests and demonstrations against the war in Vietnam; against segregation; colonialism; pollution and pesticides; education, housing and child welfare policies; capitalism and commercialism. The wind from the left kept increasing. Because of the size of the movement, it became a dictatorship that decided about both the present and the future.

Protest theater, rock concerts, lyrics, general meetings, underground papers, "happenings," and graffiti communicated the new ideas.

Communal rooms, basic furniture, and modular houses became important concepts to the movement. Design was looked upon as commercial manipulation; therefore it was given the same standardized impersonal character. Equality must be total. Everybody is your name . . .

Women kept their self-assurance, and with the growing confidence anti-fashion was born. The bra was thrown away, clothes were to be unsexy and sexless, just functional. Soft, unpressed, long pants; homecut hairstyles; and round glasses became the uniform. Anti-fashion quickly became a fashion of opinion.

Those who followed the green wave and moved to the country to self-sufficiency and a bio-dynamic culture dressed in an old-fashioned way, wearing home-sewn, home-dyed, and home-knitted clothing. Recycling and natural materials became evident.

Others became hippies and tried to forget their disappointment in an unsympathetic society by transcending the borders of the West and "normal" consciousness. Music, marijuana, and "make love not war" became part of their ideology. Everything was decorated with flowers and psychedelic arabesques. India with its ancient philosophy became a cultural center, where the new nomads wandered in search of their own values and possibly a new religion. It was also where their timeless, flowing, and decorative garments originated.

More than ever clothes marked the intentions and opinions of the movement, politically as well. But what was the result, a demonstration of nostalgia or a more just society?

The energy crisis caused uneasiness, and the idealism was diluted as civilization was put under pressure.

THROUGH CLOTHES AND ACCESSORIES one demonstrated political opinions and a desire for absolute equality between men and women.

Mah Jong's velour clothes had neither fly nor bust seam and came in unisex sizes S, M, L, and XL.

IN A VISUAL LANGUAGE that was both mythical and mystical, evocative and decorative, posters communicated the hippie's feelings. The rock band Tomorrow launched their new record *My White Bicycle* in 1967 with this poster with religious overtones.

OUTSIDE THE WESTERN WORLD hippies found ways of dressing that were untouched by the world of fashion and created their own style from what they discovered along the way.

Afghanistan, India, North Africa, and Peru came together in a colorful mixture of long skirts, sweeping shawls, shaggy fur coats, rows of jewelry, and home-dyed attic finds.

ONE DRESSED according to feelings and atmosphere, not according to etiquette and weather. A gold embroidered ankle-length velvet dress from India goes perfectly well with a fur hat.

REAL PROPERTY was considered meaningless by the young nomads. Instead, they filled their environment and their lives with cushions, pieces of cloth, unframed posters, second-hand finds—whatever could be combined into a decorative whole.

163

THE BEATLES'S RECORD *Sgt. Pepper's Lonely Hearts Club
Band* became a cult record not just through its contents.
The sleeve's cover designed by Peter Blake and Jann
Hawrith expresses the longing for the safe reliable idols and
ideals of the past.

The nostalgia in fashion, photography, interior design,
film, and advertising grew stronger and more and more commercial in the beginning of the seventies—a refuge from
the demonstrations and protests.

NATURAL MATERIALS, layer upon layer, old-fashioned patterns, shawls, earth shoes, and grandmother blouses. That was how one looked in the beginning of the seventies, whether one lived in the country or in the city. The main thing was not the place, but the ideal. The dress is from Laura Ashley.

THE IDEAL was also self-sufficiency, vegetarianism, and interiors decorated with baskets, stripped pine furniture, auction finds, old household appliances, whitewashed walls, and home-dried herbs.

Crank's in London became the first vegetarian restaurant to understand that interior design, food, and message were linked together. Replicas spread all over the world and became the beginning of a broad general awareness of the environment and the conditions under which food is produced.

OVERLEAF: The houses of the Antroposophs for the Rudolph Steiner seminar in Järna were designed by the Dane Erik Asmussen and have a functional shape, but new angles and proportions.

One of the houses, Robygge, is built from wood and painted blue, an inspiration for Post-Modernists.

WORK CLOTHES—straight-legged jeans, denim shirts, simple belts, and quilted coats and vests—quickly became fashion for all classes.

THE LOST ILLUSION, painted in 1972 by Gerhard Nordström, needs no explanation . . . .
Collection: Malmö Museum.

Back To Nature

Unemployment left its mark.

The everyday environment acquired an efficiency-oriented look that copied the factory. Interiors and exteriors revealed construction details: pipes, ventilator equipment, and machine parts. Black rubber mats, shiny steel furniture, track lighting, warehouse shelving, and sheet metal cabinets transformed the home into a workshop, while fashion designers and trend setters transformed the blue-collar worker's denim into fashion for students who wished to look as if they were manual laborers.

The body had to be kept in shape. Body building, jogging, aerobic exercises, and work-outs became religions practiced in their own churches: gyms and health clubs. Body worship manifested itself in films such as *Rocky* and through professionally marketed training clothes.

The façade was what counted, and that was true of architecture as well.

The job market was on the rise, and the desire for prestige and upward mobility was expressed in how the new money was spent. Expensive designer labels were moved to the outside of clothes exemplifying this need. And the marketers divided the consumer society into trend leaders, partisans, climbers, and imitators. Externally, the classes merged and even the differences between men and women were diminished.

Genealogy courses and antiques provided a link to the past. The family was reunited, often festively dressed as tradition prescribed. The art of cooking was given its own academies. Never before had so many museums been built. Handicrafts received a place of honor. Hand-knitted sweaters were the only good ones. Everything came back and was recycled, and architects read up on style history and created Post-Modernism. In the world of fashion, too, a high degree of classicism was felt, layered with romanticism. The strict and well-made suit became just as important as the long evening dress.

Quality of life was crucial: parquet floors, silk blouses, and an encyclopedia of one's own.

Environment no longer meant interior decoration and city planning. The green wave was proved right in the end. We must teach ourselves nature conservation.

Woman was in the center of society. She knew what she could do and who she was. Moderately curvy, rather strong, somewhat sentimental, sexy at times, often practical, a little afraid . . . Just look at her clothes. Fashion always tells the truth.

LEISURE CLOTHES became everyday wear. The fashion was inspired by the professional sports enterprises, which marked their domain with large company logos. Self absorption spread, accentuated by the Sony Walkman in 1980.

THE FAÇADE was important. Centre Pompidou in Paris was completed in 1977. It was designed by Renzo Piano and Richard Rogers and hides neither construction nor materials. The building was the first in a series of High-Tech architecture of a new honesty that became typical of the second half of the seventies.

HIGH TECH is functionalism taken directly from the warehouses and factories. Strong and clear colors, shiny metal and black rubber transformed the home into an efficient housing machine.

THE CONSTRUCTION of the clothes was also visible. The seams were on the outside, the pockets made conspicuous. Sonia Rykiel translated well the ideology of the late seventies with her yellow tricot sweater and skirt.

A DELIBERATE NEW SIMPLICITY of color as well as form, often with an essential part of the building or body clearly emphasized, spread from New York to the fashion world of Paris in the late seventies.

YVES SAINT-LAURENT knew how to handle the fundamentals of the clothes. His jacket from 1985 has the same flawless indifference to unnecessary details as the skyscrapers of New York.

EVEN THE BAG from the gift shop Oggetti in London follows the same principles.

A CLEAN SURFACE with maximum variation within a clearly defined frame. The rotor-sofa, designed by Peter Hiort-Lorenzon and Johannes Foersom, 1984, points toward flexible furniture for minimal space, something that Japan knows and which the West must learn.

JAPANESE AESTHETICS with their sacrifice of everything unnecessary and their appreciation of large clean surfaces had an enormous impact everywhere, from the way food was served to the importance of Japanese designers in the fashion industry. The coat with its kimono look is by Margit Brandt, 1986.

ONE OF THE FIRST Japanese designers in Paris was Kenzo
Takada, who introduced the layer-upon-layer look in the
seventies with a brisk mixture of folklore and Japanese
purity. Around 1980, at a time when Honda, Mitsubishi,
sushi, tempura, and bonsai entered the Western world
without losing their originality, Kenzo refined his Japanese
heritage and created severely graphic, clearly sexless clothes
for a new broad-shouldered business woman.

The pants and jacket are made of blackened, mat wool
gabardine; the shirt is white cotton.

JAPAN'S MASS-PRODUCED PACKAGING showed the same
clean simplified ideal. Shu Uemura's make-up line lacks the
insinuating cosmetic package designs of the West.

THE OBSESSION with physical fitness resulted in broader, fortified shoulders. When work-outs and jogging gave results, the fashion accentuated the muscular curves of the body.

Azzedine Alaia is one of the best trend interpreters of the eighties; he created this velour dress with black rivets in 1982.

MEMPHIS, headed by architect Ettore Sottsass, experimented with strengthened, vigorous shapes applied to well-known articles, like kettles, book shelves, or sofas.

Il Bollitore from Alessi was on the market in 1985.

KATHARINE HAMNETT'S clothes are typical of the eighties. Separately, they appear simple and not particularly striking, but put together, her combinations take on unexpected life and audacity. Therefore, the architect Norman Foster designed her boutique in London according to the same principles.

EACH ARTICLE of clothing taken separately is familiar, but combined, they create a new, highly personal and very Post-Modern whole.

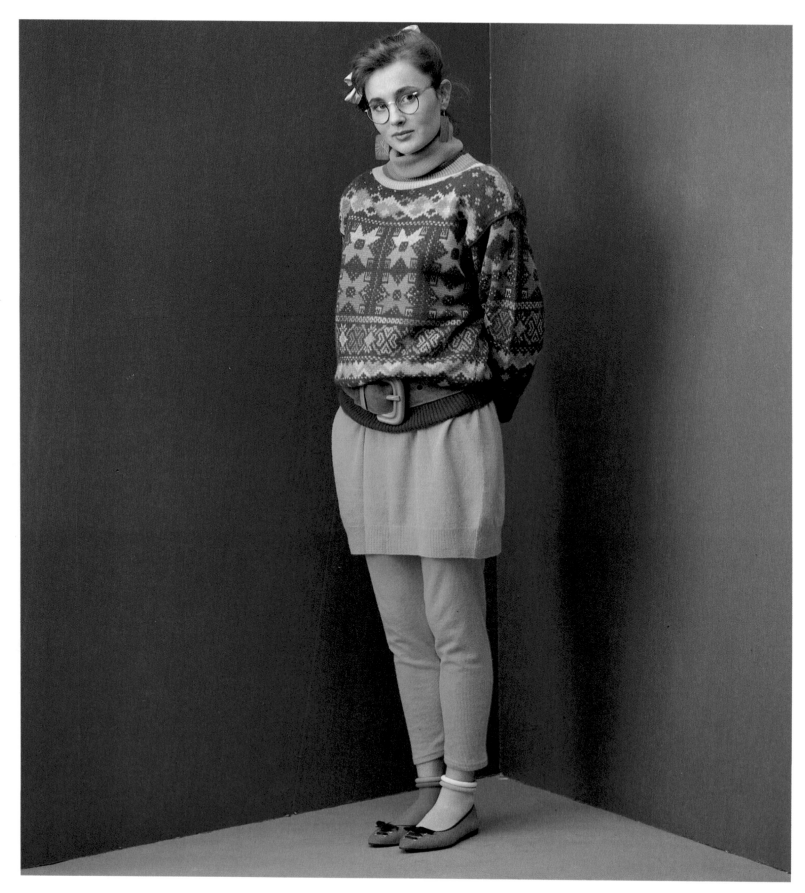

PLAYING WITH STYLES became a fashion. Basic clothes created an unexpected whole when brought together, sometimes naive, sometimes tough. Oversized sweaters, undersized skirts, multi-layers of socks, and totally unexpected accessories were the younger generation's way of showing the surrounding world that they did not trust fashion designers other than themselves.

BY WAY OF POST-MODERNISM, architecture tried to find a new freedom. Old idioms, often of a classical character, were mixed in a playful manner with the clean flat surfaces of Modernism. The proportions were unsettled without hesitation, and the choice of colors often became banal with a touch of Disneyland.

In more or less conscious expressions, Post-Modernism spread through cities and their suburbs. In Lisbon the architect Tomás Taveira was given great freedom, as he was in 1981 when he created this shopping and office center in Amoreira.

ABSOLUTE POST-MODERNISM: Hundertwasser's house in Vienna built around 1986. All styles can be found here, including a good deal of romanticism.

THE SAME MIXTURE of romanticism, functionalism, and foresight was found in Margit Brandt's fall collection of 1986.

SENSUALLY CURVY with an unexpected hollow back. The definition can be applied both to the dress and the armchair, the life-style as well as the stock market.

The armchair in glass-fiber, reinforced plastic with leather cushion was realized in 1982 by Philippe Starck for President Mitterand's study. At the same time it can be seen as a comment to power: solid front, hollow backside!

The skirts began to creep up together with the economic forecasts around 1982–83. But while the front of this dress is flat, smooth, and chaste, the back is just as empty as the president's chair. However, the fashion is accompanied by decent, tight, black stockings.

Black conservatism was the spirit of the age.

Bibliography

Ahlin, Janne. *Sigurd Lewerentz arkitekt*. Stockholm: Byggförlaget, 1985.

Arnason, H.H. *History of Modern Art*. New York: Abrams, 1986.

Bayley, Stephen. *The Conran Directory of Design*. London: Conran Octopus, 1985.

Bauhaus. Catalogue. New York: Museum of Modern Art, 1975.

Bernard, Barbara. *Fashion in the 60s*. London: St. Martin's Press, 1978.

Bony, d'Anne. *Les Années 30*. Paris: Editions du Regard, 1987.

Bourdieu, Pierre. *Kultursociologiska texter*. Lidingö: Salamander, 1986.

Brunhammar, Yvonne. *Art Deco Style*. London: Academy Editions, 1983.

Caldenby, Claës and Olof Hultin. *Asplund*. New York: Rizzoli, 1986.

Cunnington, C.W. *Feminine Attitudes in the Nineteenth Century*. London: Heinemann, 1935.

Design Source Book. London: MacDonald, 1986.

Dewey, Edvard R. *Cyklerna—Kretsloppen*. Stockholm: Liber, 1985.

Die "wilden" fünfziger jahre. Catalogue. Vienna, 1985.

Frykman and Löfgren. *Den kultiverade människan*.

Fashion 1900–1939. Catalogue. London: Victoria & Albert Museum, 1975.

Forties in Vogue. London: Conran Octopus, 1985.

Garner, Philippe. *Twentieth-Century Furniture*. Oxford: Phaidon Press, 1980.

Hartvig, Frisch. *Europas Kulturhistoria*. vol. 4. Stockholm: Wahlström & Widstrand, 1961.

Hillier, Bevis. *The Style of the Century*. New York: Dutton, 1983.

Hollander, Anne. *Seeing Through Clothes*. New York: Avon, 1975.

Howell, Georgina. *In Vogue*. Middlesex: Penguin, 1978.

Industridesign under 200 år. Specialutgåva Form till Nationalmuseums utställning. Stockholm, 1978.

Inventive Clothes 1909–1939. Catalogue. New York: The Metropolitan Museum of Art, 1973.

Johnsen, Lise. *Da moden gik amok*. Denmark: Borgen, 1983.

Julian, Philippe. *La Belle Epoque*. New York: The Metropolitan Museum of Art, 1982.

Keenan, Brigid. *The Women We Wanted to Look Like*. London: Macmillan, 1977.

Kennett, Frances. *The Collector's Book of Twentieth Century Fashion*. London: Granada, 1983.

Kron, Joan and Suzanne Slesin. *High Tech*. New York: Potter, 1978.

Laver, James. *Women's Dress in the Jazz Age*. London: Hamilton, 1964.

——*Taste & Fashion*. London: Harrarp, 1937.

——*A Concise History of Costume*. London: Thames & Hudson, 1969.

Liberty's 1875–1975. Catalogue. London, 1975.

Lucie-Smith, Edward. *Kulturen i bild*. Stockholm: Forum, 1980.

——*Art in the Seventies*. Oxford: Phaidon, 1983.

Lurie, Alison. *The Language of Clothes*. London: Heinemann, 1981.

McDermott, Catherine. *Street Style: British Design in the 80s*. New York: Rizzoli, 1987.

Meyers, William. *Imageskaparna*. Stockholm: Liber, 1986.

Norgaard, Erik. *När demerna fick ben*. Stockholm: Raben & Sjögren, 1964.

Olsson, Jan Olof. *20e århundradet*. Malmö: Forsbergs, 1965.

Poiret, Paul and Nicole Groult. *Katalog Musée de la Mode et du Costume*. Paris, 1986.

Rasmusson, Ludvig. *Fyrtiotalisterna*. Stockholm: Norstedts, 1985.

Rowland, Kurt. *A History of the Modern Movement*. London: Looking and Seeing, 1973.

Saint Laurent Yves. Catalogue. New York: The Metropolitan Museum, 1983.

Schmutzler, Robert. *Art Nouveau*. New York: Abrams, 1962.

Skivomslag. Catalogue. Stockholm: Nationalmuseum, 1982.

Sorum, Kiki. *Hollywood i moten*. Oslo: Gyldendal, 1986.

Twenties in Vogue. New York: Harmony, 1983.

Thirties in Vogue. New York: Harmony, 1985.

Traum und Wirklichkeit. Catalogue. Vienna: Küntstlerhaus, 1985.

Ward, Mary and Neville. *Home in the Twenties and Thirties*. London: Allan, 1978.

Wintzell, Inga. *Jeans och jeanskultur*. Stockholm: Nordiska Museet, 1985.

World in Vogue. London: Secker & Warburg, 1963.

Acknowledgments

Thank you for lending us clothes, accessories, objects, and interiors; answering questions, giving time and opinions; and having patience.

Without you we would not have been able to do this book:

Princess Christina, Mrs. Magnuson, Viveka and Johan Adelswüard, Lena Alvén, Marianne Andrén, Ulla Andrén, Gunnila Pennet, Ann Berntson, Margit Brandt, Margareta Büottiger, Design Center Stockholm, Gustaf Douglas, Karin Ellhammar, Rolf Elsner, Per Eklund, Margareta Eriksson, Margareta von Essen, Elisabet Fogelklou, Caroline Gyllenkrok, Erika Görander, Catherine Hamilton, Louise Hamilton, Helsingborgs Konserthus, Helsingborgs Stadsteater, Barbro Hennius, Kristina and Kalle Hessel, Margareta Hogsten, Lilavati Hüager, Gunilla Jansson, Christina Kallum, Hjördis Kristensson, Kungliga Dramatiska teatern, Maj and Johan Lachmann, Landskrona Museum, Eva Lewenhaupt, Ulla Lind, Müarit Lindstrii, Ulla Ljunggren, Amelie Lundstrüom, Margit Lundstrüom, Malmö Museum, Gunnila Mannerstråle, Christel Malmros, Inger Malmros, Millie McNaughton, Dagmar Munck af Rosenschöld, Veronica Nygren, Stina Paccini-Ohlsson, Carina Pagoldh, Rita Platzer, Caroline Reedtz-Thott, Charlotte Rydbeck, Rydebäcks Biblioteksfilial, Astrid Sampe, Lotta Schlasberg, Angelica and Erik Sparre, Malin and Gunnar Stenbeck, Elisabeth von Stockenström, Ann-Marie von Stockenström, Karin Strandberg, Birgitta Söderhielm, Elisabeth Thelander, Eva and Peder Thott, Technicrome Photographic Laboratories, Vera Thorén, Gustaf Trolle-Bonde, Mari-Ann Tornérhielm, Susan af Ugglas, Brita Wachtmeister, Eva Wachtmeister, and Kerstin Wahlgren.